The
Management Guide
to
Asserting Yourself

Kate Keenan

D0766291

Oval Books

Published by Oval Books
335 Kennington Road
London SE11 4QE
United Kingdom

Telephone: +44 (0)20 7582 7123
Fax: +44 (0)20 7582 1022
E-mail: info@ovalbooks.com

First published by Ravette Publishing, 1998
New edition published by Oval Books, 1999

Series Editor – Anne Tauté
Editor – Catriona Scott

Cover designer – Jim Wire, Quantum
Printer – Cox & Wyman Ltd
Producer – Oval Projects Ltd

Cover – Once you have learned to be
assertive you will have an enhanced
view of yourself.

Dedicated to Sue Lowe

Acknowledgement:
Angela Summerfield

ISBN: 1-902825-70-5

Contents

This book is dedicated to
those who would like to manage better
but are too busy to begin.

Asserting Yourself

Acknowledging your need to be more assertive is the first step in achieving it. Watching someone else being masterly and getting results may have made you wish you had the skills or the nerve to do the same. You can. All you need is to know how to do it.

But before you do so you need to recognise your own nature and identify the stumbling blocks that may be preventing you from becoming the assertive person you wish to be.

There are many misconceptions about what is meant by being assertive which tend to get in the way of putting it into practice. Forceful people are often thought to be exceedingly assertive simply because they have no problem in speaking up for themselves. And more timid people often labour under the false impression that assertiveness requires a degree of self-assurance they could never have. Neither is true.

This book aims to help you to become assertive through understanding the underlying issues and developing the ability to get the most out of your dealings with others.

1. Recognising Your Nature

Every individual has a predominantly **passive** or **aggressive** nature. These reactions are rather like the **default** system in a computer which is pre-set to select one or the other option, unless a conscious decision is made to alter the setting. It is worth considering the implications of this phenomenon and how they apply to your own personality.

Understanding Default Behaviour

Passive and aggressive behaviour have distinctive characteristics. These need to be understood before assertive behaviour can be developed.

- **Passive Behaviour**

  Someone whose inclination is to be passive will tend to repress their own needs and opinions. They usually submit to the will of others rather than express their own wishes.

  Passive people go to considerable lengths to avoid unpleasantness and can become extremely upset by aggressive behaviour. This includes their own, as well as other people's. When other people are aggressive, passive people tend to become even more passive to avoid exacerbating the situation.

People on the receiving end of passive behaviour often find it exasperating because they cannot establish the real needs and wishes of the passive person (for example: "Would you like tea or coffee?" "I'll have what you're having."). Passive people find that being inert suits their need to evade taking decisions and handling dissension. With passive people nothing that is not major appears sufficiently important to be worth making an extra effort for.

• Aggressive Behaviour

Someone whose inclination is to be aggressive will tend to become annoyed and confront other people when things do not go according to plan. Aggressive behaviour fuels an individual's drive and ability to achieve, but it also usually upsets others. Results can be achieved, but often the cost is high. Or nothing is achieved because others do not feel appreciated and cease to co-operate.

People on the receiving end of aggression find it difficult to understand that it is the achieving of the objective that is the main focus of the aggression, and not necessarily themselves. With aggressive behaviour, frustration is often just below the surface because the aggressor's inner needs are so passionate. And everything, whether major or minor, is worth a vigorous effort.

Becoming assertive is one way of overriding your natural default behaviour. It may seem artificial because it is not instinctive, but in fact it lies well within the range of your existing passive or aggressive behaviour.

Modifying Your Behaviour

Instinctive behaviour can be modified by exaggerating or reducing certain aspects of natural behaviour. It is this modifying process which ultimately produces assertive behaviour.

What it requires is for you to convert your natural bias into a more sophisticated response, as follows:

- **Passivity overlaid by Assertiveness**
  If you tend to be passive, you will find there is no need to go against your nature. What you need to do is toughen up, stop worrying about what other people think of you, and have the courage to express your own wants and needs.

  Modifying passive behaviour will ensure that action is taken because issues will be addressed rather than avoided. Assertiveness furnishes the mettle to present ideas which might otherwise never see the light of day, and even get you the things you have always wanted.

- **Aggression overlaid by Assertiveness**
  If you are substantially more aggressive than passive, you need to reduce your natural forcefulness by softening your approach.

  Modifying aggressive behaviour will help you to achieve your aims because people will be less aggravated and more ready to respond, yet it need not negate the motivating force which drives you. Assertiveness harnesses the passion without the negative forces of frustration and anger being present.

In each of these situations the key aspect is that which concerns the requirements of others. Passive people need to stop considering others and focus on their own requirements, while aggressive people need to stop putting themselves first and consider the requirements of others.

Advantages of Assertiveness

Assertiveness will provide the means to improve every aspect of your life, and in particular it will help you to handle difficult situations or people with finesse and competence. Once you are able to curb (if you are aggressive) or amplify (if you are passive) your behaviour you will find it much easier to:

- Impose your will in a way which gets people to take action or to alter their behaviour without resentment or rancour.

- Decline to do something in such a way that people are not offended.

- Express different (or possibly unpopular) opinions in a way which others, even if they fundamentally disagree, will find acceptable.

In addition, being assertive can help you to develop and improve the way you get on with other people. You will find that you will make the best of social situations if you are able to:

- Give and receive compliments because this enables you to develop your confidence and make others feel good about themselves.

- Put other people at ease by starting and carrying on conversations because this makes communication more enjoyable.

- Express positive feelings about other people's ideas or actions rather than keeping them to yourself because this will permit the behaviour to be affirmed on both sides.

- Admit personal shortcomings because this indicates that you are assertive and sure of yourself.

Assertive behaviour promotes equality in human relationships and gives you the flexibility to tackle different situations so that a satisfactory outcome is likely to be secured.

Summary: Being Assertive

To become assertive, a modification to the basic responses instinctive in human beings is usually required. Whether you are an innately passive or aggressive person, assertiveness will enable you to take the middle ground between the two extremes. It tempers the aggressive, and energises the passive.

Being assertive is not an end in itself, it is simply a means to an end. It is a powerful way of communicating intentions and enhancing social encounters. If you can do the unpleasant things more pleasantly and make the enjoyable things even more enjoyable, you can become the sort of person you once wanted to emulate.

Questions to Ask Yourself

Think about how you usually behave, and answer the following questions:

Passive:

▼ Do I shrink away from situations which threaten to be confrontational?

▼ Would I like to be able to express my own views more confidently?

Aggressive:

▼ Do I like to get my own way, regardless of others?

▼ Would I like to be able to influence people without upsetting them?

Both:

▼ Would I like to be able to refuse requests without feeling that I have to justify myself?

▼ Would I like my relations with other people to be more rewarding?

If you have answered 'Yes' to a number of these questions, you need to make a determined effort to assert yourself.

You Will Be Doing Better If...

★ You accept that you do not have to go against your nature to be assertive.

★ You determine to modify your natural behaviour.

★ You realise that assertiveness helps you to handle difficult situations more competently.

★ You appreciate that enjoying social situations is also part of being assertive.

★ You want to develop the skills and attitudes needed to become assertive.

2. Priming Yourself

Thoughts and feelings are the precursors to behaviour so you have to prime yourself by getting into the right frame of mind to become assertive.

As a passive person, you cannot begin to be assertive until you feel you have every right to be. As an aggressive person, you cannot become assertive until you accept that everyone else has the same rights as you do.

The priming process consists of two essential parts:

- **Knowing your fundamental assertive rights**.
- **Believing that everyone has a right to these rights.**

Fundamental Assertive Rights

There are certain assertive rights, or entitlements, for which people qualify simply by virtue of being human.

As a human being it is your right to:

- Live as pleasant a life as possible.

- Be the person you are fully and openly.

- Have opinions and express them.

- Demonstrate your feelings and emotions.

- Make mistakes. (Few people live a mistake-free life; no-one is perfect.)

- Say 'no' when you do not want to do something, without feeling apprehensive or guilty.

- Ask for what you want or need.

- Be taken account of.

- Expect decent and proper treatment.

- Choose whether or not you will get involved in certain situations or in other people's problems.

Passive people have little difficulty in acknowledging that other people have these rights, but find it more of a problem to accept that these rights also apply to themselves.

Aggressive people have little difficulty in acknowledging their own rights, but may have a problem believing that others have the same.

Whatever your basic instinct you need to believe that rights work two ways. If you expect other people to respect your rights, you must also respect theirs. If you accept 'no' from others, then you have a right to say 'no' too. If you allow other people to do things in their way, then you should be permitted to do things in your way. If you take account of other people's opinions, they should give equal consideration to yours.

Assertive rights provide a benchmark by which you can decide whether your entitlements are being ignored or whether you might be disregarding someone else's.

Believing in the Right to Have Rights

Knowing your rights is only half the picture. They are not much good to you in theory. To get the most from them, you need to believe in them.

As a **passive person**, it is essential to be convinced of your rights if you are to develop your skills in assertiveness. You have to convince yourself that you have a right to your rights. For passive people this can be difficult because they are always willing to denigrate their own rights in favour of others. Yet how can other people respect your rights if, at heart, you have difficulty believing in your right to them?

As an **aggressive person**, the pattern of behaviour is almost the inverse. You cannot transform yourself into an assertive person unless you are willing to believe that others have rights which are every bit as important as your own. For aggressive people this is not easy because they automatically expect their needs and wishes to take precedence over other people's, yet they are rarely aware that this is what they are doing.

Whatever your innate behaviour, when you believe in the right to have rights, this is what will happen:

- As a **passive person**, the more you believe your rights to be as important as everyone else's, the more confidence you will have to say what you feel, to value your judgement, to stand your ground, to expect consideration, and to be less inhibited by those who appear to be certain of themselves. And as you do, you gain in self-esteem which makes you feel much better about yourself.

- As an **aggressive person**, the more you believe in equality of rights, the more control you will exert over yourself. This means you will be much less likely to discount other people, to overlook or denigrate their views, to dominate the conversation or the situation. Instead you will start to see things from other people's points of view, be more considerate of them, and give them an opportunity to express themselves. And when you do, you will feel better about yourself.

Natural instincts can be so strong that this will need practice. It may be helpful to identify the sorts of situations where your rights should be respected and where other people's rights should be taken into account.

1. **An unwanted request**. You have been invited to an event you would rather not attend and you are bombarded with reminders.
   Your rights: To say 'no' when you do not want to do something.
   Other people's rights: To ask for what they want, and to have opinions and express them.

2. **A meal is not up to standard**. The grilled fish you ordered is uncooked and unacceptable. You are dining at a fashionable restaurant where the waiters are condescending.
   Your rights: To ask for what you want or need.
   Other people's rights: To expect decent and proper treatment.

3. **An intrusion into your leisure time**. You are reading your newspaper in the garden and your neighbour starts to play loud reggae music making it impossible for you to concentrate.
   Your rights: To live as pleasant a life as possible.
   Other people's rights: To be the person he/she is fully and openly.

4. **Equipment failure**. You have just taken delivery of expensive computer equipment in order to carry out a big project. It started and then stopped working.

Your rights: To ask for what you want or need.
Other people's rights: To be taken account of.

5. **A report is late**. A colleague has promised to send a report for 3pm. At 3.05 pm it has not arrived.
Your rights: To be taken account of.
Other people's rights: To make a mistake, and to expect decent treatment.

6. **A problem**. A friend has a problem involving someone else which is causing him or her considerable distress, and asks your advice about what to do.
Your rights: To choose whether to get involved.
Other people's rights: To demonstrate their feelings and emotions.

7. **A project**. You are at a meeting where a project is being discussed in which you are not directly concerned, but you realise that your ideas could be useful. You ask if you can give them.
Your rights: To have opinions and express them.
Other people's rights: To reject your opinion, i.e. to choose to say 'no'.

8. **A mistake**. You have double-dated yourself and cannot attend a meeting at which your colleagues expect your support.

Your rights: To make a mistake.
Other people's rights: To demonstrate their feelings and emotions.

When you accept that you have rights and that others do too, it is easier to realise when those rights are being infringed. Being aware of these rights is a very good start because it stops your initial feelings (of say, annoyance or anxiety) from blotting out the chance of handling a situation more productively.

The next stage is to learn how to use assertiveness in the pursuance of an acceptable end result – such as a report when you want it, edible food and functioning equipment.

Summary: Understanding Rights

Assertiveness is not just something that you can pick up and carry out instantly. It embodies a whole way of thinking, from the way you regard yourself to what you want from life.

You need to know that you have rights to certain entitlements and to be comfortable in claiming them. You also need to recognise that others have the same entitlements and make adjustments accordingly.

Questions to Ask Yourself

Think about how priming yourself can contribute to your becoming assertive and answer the following questions:

▼ Do I accept that, as a human being, I am endowed with fundamental rights?

▼ Do I acknowledge that others are entitled to exactly the same rights?

▼ Do I understand that I need to respect my rights and other people's?

▼ Do I recognise the various rights which can exist in different situations?

▼ Do I understand that by accepting assertive rights I have started the process of becoming assertive?

You Will Be Doing Better If...

★ You fully accept that everyone has basic assertive rights.

★ You respect these rights and remember them.

★ You believe that, in every circumstance, everyone has a right to their rights.

3. Mastering the Basic Formula

The good thing about assertiveness is that the more you do it, the more natural it will become. Going into 'assertive mode' will become part of your regular behaviour. In this way, you could say that you are assuming a role, like an actor.

As with all performances, being assertive requires that you learn your lines and get into character, so that your act seems as real to you as to the audience.

Describe, Express, Specify

There is a very simple formula for asserting yourself. It consists of remembering and doing three consecutive things. In any situation, personal or public, and whatever the circumstance (whether it relates to faulty machinery or someone failing to fulfil a function), this is what you have to do:

1) **Describe** the problem.

2) **Express** what effect this is having on you.

3) **Specify** what you want and/or what you want someone else to do to rectify the problem.

You need to memorise these three responses until they are so ingrained they become automatic.

1. Describe what the problem is

The first step is to concentrate on the facts and keep your feelings under wraps and your opinions to yourself. You need to describe the situation accurately:

- "This fish is raw in the middle", rather than "This fish is *revolting!*"
- "The report did not arrive on time."
- "Your radio is so loud that I am not able to read my newspaper."

The reason for describing the facts is that, provided they are correct, there can be no argument. This avoids any possible rows or disagreements of the kind that might ensue if you delivered an opinion.

You might think that emphasis and outrage will railroad someone into taking action, but it usually has the opposite effect. In most cases the individual receiving the brunt of your feelings is not the person responsible for the problem, but even if this is the case, it can lead to an instantly defensive reaction.

2. Express what effect this is having on you

You now have the opportunity to describe your emotions (but not to be emotional). For once in your life you have permission to tell a perfect stranger how you feel. But it does not mean that you can vent your spleen. Being assertive does not give you permission to *show* how you feel. It only gives you permission to *express* how you feel.

- "I feel disappointed and very let down, particularly as you agreed to the deadline last week."
- "I was really looking forward to an hour of perfect peace in the garden."
- "I'm extremely upset that a new computer should fail to work the very first time it's used."

All your negative feelings are valid, but what is not valid is to use abusive or explosive language, to make disparaging comments, or to strike an attitude of resigned martyrdom.

There are several degrees of insistence (or 'muscle') which you can use. You need to start off by employing the minimum level of muscle and only go on to an increased level when it fails to achieve your objectives. This is because the more strident you are, the greater the risk of provoking resistance. If the situation is serious, a more extreme form may well be appropriate, but you need to work up to it.

Here are examples of escalating levels:

I feel   – bewildered/confused *(mild)*
          – hurt/upset/distressed *(stronger)*
          – annoyed *(stronger still)*
          – angry *(extreme)*

You need to start off assuming that all intentions are good and deserve a relatively friendly, tactful and diplomatic approach. The last position, that of anger, expresses a strong verbal message and should be reserved only for a situation that really warrants it.

3. Specify what you want and/or what you want someone else to do to rectify the problem

This is how you start the process of getting some action. If you do not specify what you want, people will neither know what you want done nor, of course, be able to do it.

Your request should be specific. For example, telling your colleague that he is incompetent or unreliable because he has not delivered the report on time will not produce the report. What it will almost certainly do is create bad feeling because it is taken as a slight against his character. But stating what you want, without recrimination, should elicit the right response. For example:

- "I want your assurance that in future you will take deadlines seriously and allow yourself enough time to complete reports well before they're needed."
- "Could you please lower the volume on your radio so we can both enjoy ourselves?"

- "I need another computer delivered within one hour and I'd like your guarantee that it won't be another faulty one."

Because you are focusing on what needs to be done, it is unlikely that any negative emotion will be aroused in the person on the receiving end of your message and this makes it more likely that he or she will comply with it. And remember that whoever you are asking must also be capable of doing what you want. It is pretty ineffective to demand an instant exact replacement of the defective equipment if you know that there was a six-week delivery time on the computer in the first place.

Once you have mastered the basic approach, you may feel that a particular situation does not warrant such an unequivocal form of assertion. You may prefer to adopt a style which allows you to be more gentle without being any less assertive. For example:

- **Basic approach**: "The computer has stopped working. (Description.) "I'm extremely upset." (Expressing the effect on you.) "I need an instant replacement." (Specifying what you want.)

- **Gentler approach**: "You'll be dismayed to hear that the computer you've just delivered has stopped working. (Description.) "I'm in despair about this."

(Expressing the effect on you.) "I'd be grateful if you could let me have another computer which is capable of doing the work so that the job can be finished on time." (Specifying what you want.)

In the beginning you may not necessarily choose the right strategy to meet the circumstance, but if one strategy does not work, then trying another one may be more successful. In the end one of them should find its mark. By watching how people react, you can vary your approach. In this way you don't have to be superman or superwoman before you begin to be assertive. You can learn how to do it as you go along.

Getting into Character

Actors often say they need to get 'the walk' right or to find the right shoes to wear in order to project their 'character'. What you have to do is take on the look and demeanour of an assertive person. This means making sure that your voice and body language do not detract from sounding and appearing confident and reasonable. It is no good working at getting the words right if, when you express them, you look upset or nervous and your tone is antagonistic or apologetic.

To give an impression of being assertive you should keep calm and maintain your composure. You do this by:

- **Keeping a neutral tone of voice**. This means talking at a moderate volume and at a measured pace with no rising inflections. If you talk too softly you may be seen as timid or unconvincing, and if you talk too loudly you could easily be seen as dogmatic or disagreeable. A medium decibel level gives the impression that you are able to handle any difficulty and are not intimidated by it.

- **Using non-provocative language**. This means paying attention to how you phrase what you want to say. Provocative language alienates the listener. If, as an aggressive person, you can express yourself more in sorrow than in anger, you give the impression of someone who is approachable and reasonable in all situations. If, as a passive person, you can be as direct as you possibly can, you give the impression of someone who means what they say.

- **Looking someone in the eye when talking and listening**. This involves the other person – whether they want it or not – and gives them the impression of your being approachable and open to suggestion.

All these representations of assertive behaviour give the credibility necessary to support your message. First impressions count for a great deal, and if you can convince others that you are an assertive person in the first place, you are off to a flying start.

Summary: Assertion Skills

The core skills to assertiveness are relatively simple: they require you to present, in a neutral tone of voice and without emotion, an accurate description of the situation and your own wishes in relation to it.

Over time, these skills will become automatic and as natural to you as your own innate behaviour.

Mastering the basic formula for getting your own way (or for getting something done), is a bit like driving a car. When you are learning, there seem to be too many things to think about at the same time. But once you become proficient, it becomes so instinctive that you can scarcely recall how you arrived at your destination.

Questions to Ask Yourself

Think about mastering the basic formula and check your progress by answering the following questions:

▼ Do I know the basic formula off by heart?

▼ Do I understand that, when using the formula, I should express my feelings, but should not show them?

▼ Do I realise that it is important to start with the minimum level of insistence, and only become more persistent when other less strident pleas have failed?

▼ Do I recognise that it is essential to specify precisely what I want if anything is to be accomplished?

▼ Do I appreciate that a gentler approach can be taken when it might be more appropriate?

▼ Am I aware that how I sound and behave supports my overall credibility ?

You Will Be Doing Better If...

★ You have begun using the basic assertiveness formula.

★ You can describe the situation in factual terms.

★ You start with the minimum level of 'muscle' when
  opening the transaction.

★ You express your feelings in descriptive terms, and
  avoid showing them.

★ You state what you want to happen next in order to
  achieve a successful outcome.

★ You know that you will need to become more insis-
  tent if no results are forthcoming.

★ You are aware that a gentler approach can often be
  more effective.

★ You appreciate that to be perceived as an assertive
  person, *how you say* something is as important as
  what you say.

4. Enlarging Your Repertoire

The basic approach to being assertive can achieve a great deal. However, you need to be equally assertive when faced with unexpected or awkward situations, particularly those which involve a degree of conflict. This is especially necessary in situations where you know your opinions are likely to be unpopular, where you consider the request being made of you is unreasonable, or where you want someone to behave differently.

There are five classic routines which you need to add to your repertoire. Each enables you to assert yourself in an appropriate way.

Impersonating Mr. Spock

This is useful when faced with aggression, hostility, or opinions with which you disagree. The stratagem is to neutralise your opponents' emotion and momentum, with a logical response rather than retaliating in the same style (e.g. "That's a stupid thing to say") or making no response at all.

The way to do this is to answer in a dispassionate and rational manner. This has a remarkably disconcerting affect on the aggressor. Good standby lines would be:

- "That's an interesting point of view, could you give me some reasons as to how you arrived at it?"
- "I'd like to suggest we try to be more constructive."
- "We obviously have a problem which we need to resolve."
- "What would you like me to do about this?"

The more 'Mr. Spock'-like you can remain, the more the other person's aggression will weaken, and the more he or she will be obliged to come round to your unemotional approach.

Becoming a Broken Record

This is mainly used when others want to impose their will on you. In this instance you need to pick one unassailable reason why you cannot comply, and stick to it. The more the other person tries to convince you to do something or to get round you, the more you need to keep repeating the same phrase over and over again, like a broken record.

What it involves is going from point 1 to point 3 like a needle stuck in a groove. For example:

1. 'You simply must come to the meeting.'
   "I'd like to, but I have another appointment."
2. 'But I was counting on you being there!'
   "Unfortunately, I can't change my other appointment."

3. 'Everyone will be very disappointed.'
   "So will I, but it's a date that can't be changed."

The technique is to give one sound reason as to why you cannot fall in with the other person's requirements. Your intention is to get that person to accept your needs or wishes. The more the insistence, the more you repeat what you said at the start, though not necessarily using the same words.

There is one important thing to remember: it is crucial to avoid diluting your argument. So give only one or, at the most, two reasons. If you offer too many (even if they are all relevant and valid), your weakest one will be picked up and used against you.

The more you can stick in your groove, the more people will realise that you are impervious to coercion. When they realise they are not getting anywhere, they usually capitulate. And you will feel good because you have got your way by remaining unruffled throughout.

Imitating a Crab

When someone makes a vindictive or vicious remark, you may find that stepping sideways like a crab is your best policy. Because there is often no adequate answer you can give which allows you to assert yourself, you should just dodge the barb altogether.

For example:

'Is it too much to ask for you to get here on time?'
"Isn't it a lovely day?"

'So what are you going to do to sort this mess out?'
"I'd like to think about that."

You need not of course respond at all – simply make direct, intentional and deliberate eye contact with the person trying to bait you, while offering no reply. Using the silent treatment by saying nothing can be particularly effective on the telephone.

The side-step is a better ploy than it might at first appear. Nobody can gainsay silence, nor a cheerful remark that has nothing to do with the issue. However heated an attack, if you refuse to be drawn, it has to peter out.

Playing the 'I' Game

This is a useful technique when someone else's behaviour is affecting you. You need to remember that no-one can make you feel a certain way: rather, it is you who chooses to feel the way you do. The instinctive thing to do is to blame the person whose words or actions are provoking your feelings, e.g: "You've upset me"/"You've ruined my day". However, the use of 'You' puts the other person in the role of culprit, which raises the emotional temperature.

Instead, what you have to do is quietly and firmly state the effect that someone's words or actions are having on you, by using the word 'I':

- "I have to say I find that remark very hurtful/ distressing."
- "I'm most upset by what has happened."
- "I'm finding this conversation very difficult to take."

This expression of your feelings lets people know the effect their behaviour is having on you which they may not have realised (particularly if the conversation is on the telephone). It usually results in bringing someone up short because it forces them to consider how they are behaving. It is not only disarming, it tends to prevent an escalation of unpleasantness, and offers an opportunity to change course.

Simulating Empathy

This is used when someone else's action, or lack of action, has caused you a problem. No matter how annoyed (as an aggressive person) or inhibited (as a passive person) you might feel, if you make the other person feel that he or she counts, you will involve that person in your predicament, simply because you are acknowledging theirs.

What you do is use an empathic approach, one which recognises some of the difficulties others might be facing:

- "I know how extremely busy you are…"
- "I am only too aware of the problems you have had with your supplier…"
- "I do appreciate that you are doing your best…"
- "I do understand the difficult position you are in…"

The more you can demonstrate that you are aware of the pressures or difficulties others are experiencing, the more likely you are to elicit the response you want, and even to achieve their willing compliance.

Summary: Defusing Difficulties

To cope competently with conflict you need to assert yourself in a way which sets out to defuse and smooth. Deflecting antagonism, resisting blandishments, declining to engage in argument, expressing your feelings and showing empathy are all assertive methods of dealing with challenging situations.

The techniques you can choose to adopt vary according to the circumstances in which you find yourself. Selecting appropriate tactics from your repertoire and improvising when necessary allows you to handle or neutralise the behaviour of others.

Questions to Ask Yourself

Think about the repertoire available to you when asserting yourself and answer the following questions:

▼ Do I recognise that responding unemotionally can avoid confrontation?

▼ Do I understand how applying the broken record technique will prevent my being bulldozed into doing something?

▼ Am I aware that side-stepping an issue can get me out of hostile encounters?

▼ Do I appreciate that by expressing my feelings directly, a situation can be tempered because people are informed of the effect of their behaviour?

▼ Do I realise that if I make other people aware that I understand their problems, it is easier for me to request them to do something?

▼ Do I acknowledge that there are many different ways of being assertive?

You Will Be Doing Better If...

★ You assess the situation and decide which approach may be appropriate.

★ You defuse others' emotions by taking a rational approach.

★ You prevent yourself being coerced by repeating your refusal politely and insistently.

★ You side-step provocative remarks.

★ You are prepared to state directly how you feel when a situation gets heated.

★ You empathise with other people before stating calmly what you would like them to do.

★ You are aware that you have a range of techniques to choose from when being assertive.

5. Adding to Your Social Skills

Developing your social skills is another aspect of asserting yourself. Being able to achieve objectives is a very different thing to getting on well with people, yet the same social skills are part and parcel of achieving objectives assertively. And, like a diamond, the more facets you present, the more people will associate assertive behaviour with you as a person.

Paying and Accepting Compliments

Paying compliments does not happen as often as it should. You may think that someone looks exceptionally smart, or that their work is first rate, but you do not put those thoughts into words – perhaps because you think it is obvious, or because you think the recipient would not welcome your opinion.

It will encourage you to express your thoughts if you remember that everybody likes a compliment – however they may react. No-one is so confident that they do not value another person's good opinion.

This means that the occasional negative response should not deter you from paying further compliments either to the same person or to others.

The way you deliver a compliment is as much a part of it as what you say. Use a clear, confident voice, preferably looking directly at the person: "What a wonderful colour you're wearing"/"You've made a marvellous job of this document".

If you think positive, assertive thoughts about someone and do not communicate them, you deny yourself a valuable social skill which, as well as making other people feel good about themselves, increases your own self-assurance.

Accepting compliments in an assertive manner is something which may also need to be learned. For instance, if at a function someone says out of the blue, "I do like what you're wearing" and in return gets a dismissive comment from you – "Oh, this old rag/old thing. I've had it for ages" – it's the equivalent of being struck by a wet fish. A simple, "Thank you. I'm glad you like it" indicates that the compliment is appreciated and gives the speaker a sense of his or her opinion being valued.

Conversing More Easily

Taking an assertive stance in conversation helps you not only to forge new relationships, but gets you out of sticky situations. Some people find it daunting to talk to a complete stranger in a social situation, so they tend to hang back and wait for someone else to make all the effort. Others take over and do not let anyone get a word in edgewise.

Knowing how to approach people on your own and how to start, then continue, a conversation are all part of the assertive package that you need to acquire and use to your advantage.

The Approach

You need an introductory gambit which will fit any occasion, e.g: "Hello, I don't think we've met. I'm Chris Collier."/"May I introduce myself. My name is…"

The Start

The easiest way to get conversation flowing is to ask a question. It does not have to be anything profound. It is simply a 'hook' to get started. For example: "Have you been to an event of this kind before?" The good thing is that no matter how artificial this may seem at first, you will inevitably become interested in the ensuing dialogue.

The Continuation

To keep the conversational ball going back and forth, continue to ask questions, in particular ones which elicit opinions, such as "What do you think of today's news about… ?"/"How do you feel about the new plan to… ?" Remember that most people like being asked their opinion, and they are equally glad to talk about themselves and their experiences.

This is a more productive approach than the one people frequently use – known as 'a leading question' – which asks for agreement to their own opinions, e.g. "Don't you think it's terrible that... ?"/"This is a good idea, isn't it?"

Questions perform the role of catalyst. They save you having to rack your brain for things to say. They also give you a chance to control the conversation by listening attentively to the answers and asking further questions about what has been said. Questions are flattering because they encourage others to think they must be interesting if you are asking, and to feel that you must be interested if you are listening.

Expressing Positive Feelings

At times you may think that someone has done something worthwhile or has made a brave stand about an issue. Just thinking this is not enough. If you do not articulate the good thoughts you are thinking, they cannot have an effect. It is not much use to wish later on that you had said something, particularly when you find out that it could have been helpful, either to the proceedings or to a person.

To be assertive, you need to make your feelings known. "I admired the mature way you accepted the group view, even when it didn't coincide with your own."/"I was most impressed with how you handled that awkward situation."

Letting people know when you think they have done something worthy of comment is a simple and effective way to cement relationships. It not only increases other people's sense of worth, it will make you feel good to have expressed positive feelings.

Admitting Shortcomings

Many people think it is an admission of weakness to admit to not understanding something, not knowing something, or not being able to do something. This is not the case. In fact, it is a very assertive thing to do.

In all likelihood, others may feel the same but may be reluctant to admit their own failing. For example, if you say, "I've never been good at figures, so could you explain them to me in simple terms", you give others the chance to admit similar imperfections with impunity.

Open admissions of one's foibles and frailties are indicative of an assertive person (someone who does not mind what others think). Defensive people would never admit their shortcomings. If you can develop the confidence to acknowledge your inadequacies, you let others know that you are just as flawed as everyone else. This encourages people to feel more at ease in your company and more open in their dealings with you.

Summary: Behaving Constructively

Whether by nature you tend to take the lead or are inclined to take a back seat, acknowledging and offering compliments as well as expressing good opinions and engaging in conversation are constructive ways of adding to your social skills.

All are aspects of assertive behaviour and each prompts other people to respond positively in return.

Questions to Ask Yourself

Think about your relationships with others and answer the following questions:

▼ Do I understand the part that paying others compliments plays in being assertive?

▼ Do I appreciate that accepting compliments courteously makes the other person feel valued?

▼ Do I realise that opening a conversation is relatively easy?

▼ Do I understand that asking questions is a good way to continue and develop the conversation?

▼ Am I prepared to express my positive feelings when someone has done something worthwhile?

▼ Am I happy to admit my shortcomings?

▼ Do I understand that relating positively to others in social situations is an integral part of being an assertive person?

You Will Be Doing Better If...

★ You work at paying people compliments instead of just thinking nice things.

★ You are gracious when others pay you compliments.

★ You have developed some simple strategies for opening conversations.

★ You use the 'What/How' type of question to get informative answers.

★ You let people know when you value what they have said or done.

★ You are prepared to admit your shortcomings, especially when it will further the proceedings.

★ You recognise the role that being assertive plays in cementing relationships.

6. Your Attitude to Assertion

Adopting an assertive way of doing things means that you are able to make your own choices. You have taken control of yourself, rather than allowing those around you either to take you over or to be dominated by you. But you may need occasionally to stiffen your resolve.

Strengthening Your Beliefs

Becoming assertive requires you to strengthen the beliefs you hold about your rights and other people's. You may have accepted in an intellectual sense that everyone has entitlements, but on an emotional level you may not yet be completely convinced.

As a formerly **passive person**, others will still expect you to be at their beck and call, so you need to make sure you do not slip back into negative thoughts. For example, when asked to do something you would rather not do, instead of thinking "X is sure to dislike me if I refuse" you should say to yourself "I have the right to refuse". The more you do this, the more you will believe it.

But you still need to beware of allowing yourself to be worn down. Having refused once, you must not lessen your new-found assertiveness by giving in to a request at the second or third time of asking.

As a formerly **aggressive person** others will still expect you to discount or override their opinions and views, so you need to keep focusing on the fact that it is easier to achieve things when others are with you rather than against you. And they are more likely to show willing or be co-operative if you elicit their thoughts and ideas.

Everyone has the right to exercise their rights without infringing those of others. And you need to strengthen your belief in this premise from time to time if you are not to backslide.

Handling Others' Reactions

Your newly-developed style of doing things can sometimes prove to be more of a problem for others than it is for you. It is useful to be aware of possible reactions you may encounter from others to your new-found assertiveness.

As a formerly **passive person**, you may never have been viewed as a person with needs or opinions. So when you suddenly metamorphose from a passive person into one who is no longer backward in coming forward, others may be tempted to think, "Who does he think he is?", or "All of a sudden she's taking over" because they find your confidence unexpected and challenging.

And because they can no longer dismiss you, people may behave aggressively towards you in an attempt to regain lost dominance.

As a formerly **aggressive person**, once you decide to curtail your behaviour, others may not know how to react. They will be expecting to be dominated as before and, while they may not have liked it, at least they knew what to expect. They may be confused by your new approach. They may even resent having to make decisions for themselves, rather than simply agreeing to yours.

It is helpful to be alert to the range of reactions which may arise simply because you have become an assertive person. However, now that you have the skills to respond and reduce negative reactions from other people – use them.

Choosing to be Unassertive

Knowing how to be assertive gives you the option to choose not to be. On some occasions, it could be more appropriate to adopt a subtle approach.

You always have the option to decide not to be assertive in circumstances where the incident is either:

a) too trivial and not worth fighting for, or

b) too alarming not to back away from.

Choice is an essential part of the process because it should not lead you into more difficulties. It should lessen them.

Keeping Going

Modifying one's behaviour is usually hard work; it only comes with practice and in small steps. Because of this you should not be put off by the fact that it may take time before you see results. This is a skill for life and cannot be achieved overnight. So be content to get more proficient with each opportunity and take measured strides towards achieving your aim.

Remember that you are working with a valuable resource – yourself – and it is incumbent upon you to look after this personal asset very carefully. There are no magic answers; assertiveness may not work every time, but it certainly beats the alternatives.

For a formerly **passive person** the fact that it works and that you now find you are able to get your way may be fairly intimidating. For a formerly **aggressive person** the patience required may test you to the limit, and may invite you to take an aggressive line once more because it requires so much less effort or forethought.

But, whichever your natural inclinations, never be tempted to revert to old ways.

Summary: The Joys of Assertiveness

Behaving in an assertive manner requires you to accept a whole philosophy about who you are and what rights you and other people possess as human beings.

Believing in your entitlements involves adapting your thoughts and modifying deep-rooted, instinctive behaviour. You need to be aware of how these changes may affect those who have known the non-assertive person you once were. And you need to keep going no matter what surprising reactions you encounter – even your own.

Assertiveness is a skill which allows you to stand up for your rights in an appropriate manner, express your feelings, reach out to others and build equal relationships.

Most importantly, it is the one means by which you can become the person you want to be.

Questions to Ask Yourself

Think about your attitude to being assertive and answer the following questions:

▼ Do I realise I may have to strengthen my belief in my assertive rights from time to time?

▼ Am I resolved not to be discouraged by the responses others may demonstrate when I put my assertiveness into practice?

▼ Am I prepared to act assertively when encountering these reactions?

▼ Do I appreciate that there are times when it might be prudent not to be assertive?

▼ Am I aware that being assertive may take time to develop and that I will always be learning?

▼ Do I realise that being assertive forms part of the whole philosophy of understanding who I am?

You Will Be Doing Better If...

★ You remind yourself every so often of your basic assertive rights.

★ You recognise that other people may be less pleased about your becoming assertive than you are.

★ You appreciate that there are some circumstances when being assertive may not be the best choice to make.

★ You realise that it will take time (probably most of the rest of your lifetime) to become proficient in asserting yourself.

★ You are aware that being assertive enables you to become the person you always really wanted to be.

Check List for Asserting Yourself

If you are finding that being assertive is proving less easy than you thought, consider whether this is because you have failed to take account of one or more of the following aspects:

Priming Yourself

Should asserting yourself seem more daunting than you expected, you may not have fully accepted that you have entitlements (if you are naturally passive) or that others have them too (if you are naturally aggressive). Perhaps you are finding it difficult to believe that these rights are fully applicable to you and so do not take them on board. Or maybe you find it less easy to see things from other people's points of view and so fail to give them the opportunity to express themselves.

Learning to be Assertive

If you are finding it difficult to tackle situations assertively, it may be that you have not been using the basic formula (Describe/Express/Specify) enough for it to have become second nature to you. You may have let your feelings overwhelm you rather than focussing on the outcome you desire. Possibly it is simply that you are not giving a convincing enough imitation of an assertive person in your manner and tone.

Enlarging Your Repertoire

If you find that challenging situations still tend to make you overreact – by dodging the issue (passive) or exploding (aggressive) – you are probably not using the routine best suited to the situation. You need to develop the whole range of techniques for asserting yourself so that you can select the right one to match the circumstances, or try each of them in turn (like fitting the correct key in a lock) until one or other works.

Adding to Your Social Skills

If you think that you are not making the best of the social situation in which you find yourself, you may not have appreciated that the amount of effort you expend is directly related to your effectiveness. You may need to take a more active part by asking questions and giving opinions in such a way that others cannot help but respond favourably.

Your Attitude to Assertion

If you find yourself backing off from being assertive, and reverting to type, it may be that you have not entirely accepted the assertiveness philosophy. You need to remind yourself that so long as you respect the rights of others, you have every right to enjoy the advantages afforded to you by being assertive.

The Benefits of Asserting Yourself

Once you understand the power that being assertive can bestow on you, your life will become a lot more productive.

For the **passive** person the benefits of overcoming passivity are that:

- You will prevent others from riding roughshod over you.

- You will find it easier to ask people to do things and so get things done.

- You will gain self-confidence and therefore get more from your relationships with others.

- You will be comfortable expressing your opinions and getting your viewpoint accepted by others.

- You will feel you count, which makes you feel good about yourself.

- You will be able to say 'no' and mean it. What is more, you will be able to stick to it, and not give in when pressed.

For the passive person, once assertiveness has been learned, self-esteem and self-assurance will increase.

For the **aggressive** person, the benefits of replacing aggression with assertion are that:

- You will get things done in a calmer and less frenetic way.

- You will use up less energy striving for your goals.

- You will feel less frustrated.

- You will get much more from those who work with you because you will be respecting their rights.

- You will have more time to spend on yourself, rather than spending time chasing others.

- You will learn a lot more because you will listen more and so understand others better.

- You will be more able to do what you want because you will get co-operation from other people.

Becoming assertive is not a mysterious gift. It is an attitude of mind and a series of skills. Once you have acquired these and have begun to put them into practice, day-to-day activities become much easier.

Assertive behaviour does more than achieve your wishes in terms of your dealings with others. It also makes you feel good about yourself.

Glossary

Here are some definitions in relation to Asserting Yourself.

Aggressive behaviour – Quarrelsome or belligerent behaviour which gives vent to thoughts and feelings and denies the rights of others. What is generally, but wrongly, thought to be assertive.

Passive behaviour – Submissive and acquiescent behaviour which bottles up thoughts and feelings and denies personal rights.

Assertive behaviour – Rational and authoritative behaviour which strikes the right note and does not deny anyone's rights.

Belief – Conviction which needs strengthening when the going gets tough.

Compliment – A socially acceptable way of showing admiration.

Confrontational situations – Those which most need an assertive response.

Conversation – Friendly inquisition under the guise of putting people at their ease.

Default – The pre-programmed system to which behaviour will revert if assertiveness is not enacted.

Empathy – The ability to put yourself in someone else's shoes.

Feelings – Emotional reactions which can get in the way of being assertive, but which, if described unemotionally, can help you to be assertive.

Formula – An effective prescription for getting what you DESire: Describe, Express, Specify.

Instincts – Inborn tendencies to behave in a non-assertive way.

Modifying – Making small but significant alterations.

Priming Yourself – Mental workout to develop the fitness to be assertive.

Questions – Sparks to set conversation alight.

Rights – Freedoms or powers due to you and which need to be respected in others.

Repertoire – The stock of techniques that help you to take control of confrontational situations.

Shortcomings – Inadequacies which, when admitted, can make you seem anything but inadequate.

Social Skills – Means for getting on with people, much enriched by being assertive.

The Author

Kate Keenan is a Chartered Occupational Psychologist with degrees in affiliated subjects (B.Sc., M.Phil.) and a number of qualifications in others.

She founded Keenan Research, an industrial psychology consultancy, in 1978. The work of the consultancy is fundamentally concerned with helping people to achieve their potential and make a better job of their management.

By devising work programmes for companies she enables them to target and remedy their managerial problems – from personnel selection and individual assessment to team building and attitude surveys. She believes in giving priority to training the managers to institute their own programmes, so that their company resources are developed and expanded.

As someone inclined to passive behaviour, she has always preferred to say nothing than risk ructions of any kind. However, assiduous application of the assertion formula and a passable performance of Mr. Spock and the Broken Record have allowed her to be taken for an assertive person for most of her life.

THE MANAGEMENT GUIDES

'Especially for people who have neither the time nor the inclination for ploughing through the normal tomes...'

The Daily Telegraph

These books are available from your local bookshop in the UK, or from the publishers:

Oval Books, 335 Kennington Road, London SE11 4QE
Telephone: (0) 20 7582 7123; Fax: (0) 20 7582 4887;
E-mail: info@ovalbooks.com

The Management Guides are also available from the publishers on audio cassette, and in electronic form for PDAs.